The Sanctuary of Belonging

Poems by Ellen Grace O'Brian

Center for Spiritual Enlightenment

The Sanctuary of Belonging

Illustrations by Victoria Willis
Cover and book design by Clarice Hirata, Hirata Design
Cover photograph of the author by Michael Scott

ISBN   0-9660518-1-5

Center for Spiritual Enlightenment
Post Office Box 112185
Campbell, California 95011-2185
408-244-5151
email: cse@best.com

To Sri Satya Sai Baba,

Embodiment of Love

With appreciation for my husband Michael who hears the poems with his heart and for Aminah who encouraged me to make the journey.

We've come into the presence of the one

who was never apart from us.

■ Rumi

Contents

Introduction

In January of 1997, I decided to follow my heart's inclination to journey to the ashram of Sri Satya Sai Baba in Puttaparthi, a village in South India. These poems (with the exception of numbers one and thirteen) were written there. They are all inspired by his holy presence and offered to him with love and in deepest gratitude. Any light that shines in them is through his grace.

The illustrations in this book by Victoria Willis are witness to a collaboration of love that occurs through such grace. Victoria and I were two strangers traveling the same path. We ended up as roommates in Puttaparthi. Each day as we sat among the devotees at Baba's ashram awaiting his darshan, we worshipped in our own way. Independent of one another, I would write poems, and she would sketch. Some months later when I decided to publish the poems, I contacted Victoria to see if any of her sketches might be appropriate for the book. Her willingness to participate in the project, the beautiful synchronicity of the words and images, and the ease with which it came together was a teaching in itself for me. I have heard it said that when Spirit wants to do something, It will bring together the people and the resources necessary to make it happen. Although I have witnessed this truth many times in my life, never before has it been quite so sweet.

May the sweetness of this book's devotion touch your heart, may it awaken within you remembrance of the One to Whom all praises are sung.

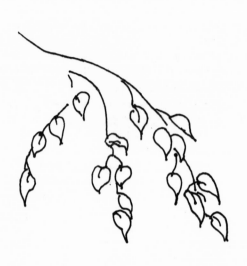

O N E

Even the hummingbird stops
at noon to pray
offering the ruby
of praise, the price
of one moment
in the green sanctuary
of belonging.

T W O

Before dawn I walk
the cool streets
the first fires of morning
burn, already
the women have touched
their foreheads
with the color

of your love.
They move toward you
like brides
their hearts
the bouquets
they carry
fragrant with desire
for you.

They have left
their homes
travel without money
seek
only you,
swift
as birds.

THREE

I've been listening
to the sound of your footsteps:
birds coming in to roost
rose petals opening
foam of the wave
disappearing in sand.

The women who are asleep
miss the colors of dawn
and the sound of you
coming to meet them.

FOUR

Hari, those rose letters
penned on azure skies
you slipped daily at dawn
under the door

of my mind
have called me from my home.
Why hide from me now?
Their fragrance still speaks.

When night jasmine
fills the air
I know: not even
the darkness escapes
your call to bloom.

FIVE

Shiva
hands me a flower
then, a few leaves.
I tell her,
"I have nothing
to give."
She says: "Tomorrow.
Remember
my name
is Shiva."

SIX

My heart is heavy
with its own demand,
I can hardly breathe.
I try to shake it off
but it waits, like Penelope
tying together the
strands of your absence.

Inside the lamp
still burns. It
demands your return
by refusing to go out.

SEVEN

I've been dreaming I'm an orphan.
Always, it's the same dream.
Long tables and many children
there is food
but I do not eat.
I am feeding
on my secret: any moment
the door will open and
You will come for me.
Later, riding through
the green countryside,
I will not look back.

To keep his donkey close by
the merchant ties
its front legs together.
Now it cannot wander
this donkey can be trusted
near his neighbor's carrots.
The merchant is free to work

all day without worry.
At dusk, he unties this
tendency to wander and
together, they go home.

I tie the mischief of my mind
with the rope of your name.
It's dusk and I'm waiting
for you. Untie the knot
Let's go home.

NINE

Mother you have shown the doves
where and how to build their nests
in the temple eaves.
I am a lost one,
the generation
who did not learn to sew,
the recipes of my grandmothers
are gone.
I left that house.
Now you
must show me
the simple
weaving together
of the soul life.

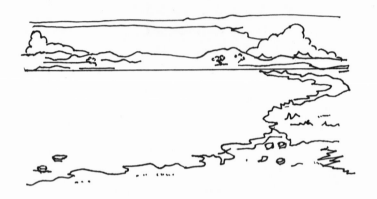

TEN

In the shadows
the mud jumps!
A wet frog
alive with you, sings
even before dawn.
My heart leaps
knowing
you
may appear
like that.

ELEVEN

All this way I traveled
for one look in your eyes, the one
that will change my life.
I sit on the ground
of my need and wait
for the rising of the sun.

The other girl, the one
who did not
catch your eye,
has left.
She pretends to be
light hearted, free
of the awful waiting.
She says her teachers
are gone and she
is alone.
Hers is a freedom

I do not want.
The one I want
is the freedom
of the heart gates
swinging open
and you
walking through.

TWELVE

Hari, what can win you?
I have been circling
around you for days
breathing your name.

Beauty means nothing to you
the only jewels you want
come from your own hands.

I watch the monkeys
circle the holy shrine
follow each other
head tail back again
sliding down
Krishna's body
with ease.

THIRTEEN

In the heart
is a well, filled
with the sound
of silence.
Drink

from it.
One taste
changes everything.

How do I know?
The day I stopped

sitting on the edge
and fell in,
told me this.

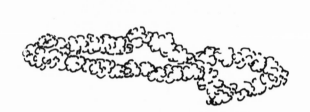

FOURTEEN

I cannot use
what you have given me.
When I try to give it
away, it returns.
They do not want it
in the marketplace. There
the flower vendors tie
the white flowers together
for other women's hair.
I am uncovered
unadorned
I wear
only that.

FIFTEEN

I have not told
the other women
how you met me
in that secret place
and made the honey drip.
So many of them tell
lies about you,
your name rolls
off their tongues.
Before we met I could
talk with them, now
I am mute.
After meeting you
everything I say
is a betrayal.

Notes on the Illustrations

The sketches in the text were created by free lance artist Victoria Willis. With the exception of number fifteen (which is taken from a statue in the author's collection), all of the sketches are drawn from the environment of the village of Puttaparthi in South India and the sacred architecture of Prashanti Nilayam, the ashram of Sri Satya Sai Baba.

Victoria's sketches are a meditative process, expressing the formless experience of Spirit through capturing the beauty of the physical surroundings.

Index of First Lines

Other Books by Ellen Grace O'Brian

Living the Eternal Way
Spiritual Meaning and Practice for Daily Life

One Heart Opening
Poems for the Journey of Awakening
(also available on audio cassette)

For information about the teaching schedule of the author, or to receive a schedule of spiritual programs and retreats offered by the Center, contact:

Center for Spiritual Enlightenment
Post Office Box 112185
Campbell, California 95011-2185
Telephone: (408) 244 - 5151
email: cse@best.com